All Kinds
Babies

Linda M. Washington

Here is a mother bird.

Here is her baby.

Here is a mother cat.

Here is her baby.

Here is a mother dog.

Here is her baby.

Here is a mother sheep.

Here is her baby.

Here is a mother cow.

Here is her baby.

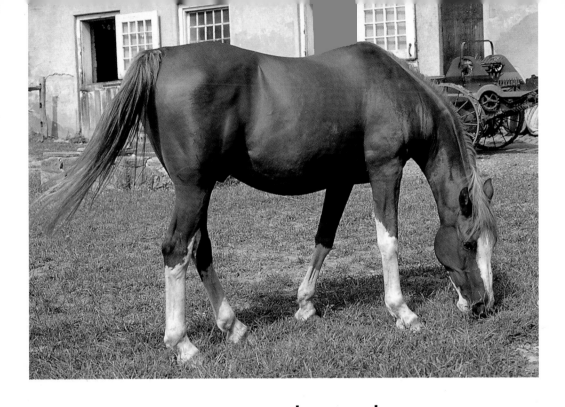

Here is a mother horse.

Here is her baby.

Here is a mother whale.

Here is her baby.

Here is a mother.

Here is her baby.